ALLAN YOUNGER
THE DARK SIDE

ALLAN YOUNGER
THE DARK SIDE

Publihsed by BooxAi
ISBN: 978-965-577-902-8

THE DARK SIDE

ALLAN YOUNGER

CONTENTS

A FATHERS' LOVE

Listened to a song today – can't get the lyrics out of my mind.
They fly around and won't go away,
soaring high inside my head seems unfair to be emotion led.
A song about fathers and of their sons.
Of pain and anguish over loved ones – you want them like you,
just as you are, but be honest did you really go far?
Were you like your father or did you break free?
Did you ask yourself where would you rather be?
You made the mold and fashioned the clay,
but what of your ego, did you have it your way?
Did you tell him you loved him when he was a child?
Did you show him your love, did you let it run wild?
That being a man is about caring and crying, and if you want
then you can?
So, on goes the music around in my head along with the tears
as well as old fears.
Does he know that I love him as he walks away?
I whisper it softly but I know he can hear when his pace starts
to slow and he looks back with no fear.
He seems to be saying 'Don't worry Dad I'm on the right track.
I know that you love me – one day I'll be back.'
It's what I said to my father as well, so now I just wait for time
to tell.

FLOTSAM AND JETSAM

I lie in the dark eyes open
My eyes, like a man hanging desperately from the edge of a cliff, grab at the light trying to focus as if....
But there is no light save that in my head growing ever brighter then suddenly dead.
My eyes greet the dark of the night.
I lie in the dark eyes open
In the dark of the night, time creeps so slow – forever lingering, refusing to go.
Ever loud, the beat of my heart fills my ears.
Cold blood flows, visits old friends – awakens old fears then slowly but surely brings on my tears.
Like flotsam and jetsam in rivers flow, memories surface then sink with nothing to show.
I know they were there but where did they go?
I lie in the dark eyes open
I remember my love – taste the salt in my tears.
We ruled the world, had perfect years.
Then I sigh as I welcome the warmth of the sun as with one final breath, I go forward to meet her as we become one.
Finally,
I lie, eyes closed.

LEAF

Spring calls. I rise from my slumber, exhilarated by the sounds as life awakens.
On my tree.
I look around and see many friends. All of us young and eager but where are the others?
Those with the experience of yester year, they have gone – vanished as if never here.
In the gentle sun I stretch and glory with all my friends to live my story.
But what will happen when I too gain the experience of yester year?
Will someone greet me, or will I just fall to vanish as if never here at all.

80

It took a long time to get here.
I started down my road eighty years ago, and here I am.
Remember as remember can.
Don't let them tell you time passes quickly, it has taken me eighty years to get here, and I savor every moment like a fine wine or perhaps a nice piece of chocolate.
Takes me back to my childhood, my favorite treat.
Memories, waiting to be teased from my mind, each one to grab onto, to slowly unwrap.
They wait patiently as I summon them one by one.
No pushing or shoving, they just wait their turn.
I roll the fine wine – my chocolate around in my mouth then let it linger and slip off my tongue just like my memories one by one.
They stay in my mind, going around and around till I let them run free.
A hint of what was? – I know they were there.
Problem is, I can't always catch them, so unfair.
It feels so unkind as they tease my mind for what, more memories hiding behind?
So many to choose from but they refuse to come out 'till, like old autumn leaves blowing around,
I pick them up quickly as if from the ground.
Some, old withered leaves that crumble to dust as I grab them too tight, but I'm afraid they'll escape like thieves in the night.
I promise myself when spring comes along to tidy my head, sort out my memories, put them to bed.

To throw out the junk – my smiles, my laughter, my tears and old fears so patiently gathered over 80 good years.
But I've tried before and stopped when I saw that my memories are me, years of laughter and sunshine and many good times.
Of passion and loving and nursery rhymes.
Memories of children when they were born, taking first steps as they made their own way.
Can I give it all up? Never not even for one extra day.
I'm sorry but I can't bear to part with any of them. Why should I?
They are the essence of me, without them a mere shadow; eyes that don't see.
So, if I forget your name that's alright, I might just remember during the night.
I won't be asleep for there's too much to do, reliving my life before it all passes through.

MEMORIES

Crack of whip shredding air.
Crack of gunshot ringing out.
Crack of ice as glacier hits water below.
None of these hurt like the crack of my tree as it slowly surrendered to the weight of the snow.
It hurt as memories poured from its trunk, sap slowly being sucked into the ground.
They fade as I run to gather them up – memories flying like leaves blown around.
I remember when I climbed my tree, the hero no one could stop as I claimed my place at the very top.
My initials carved into the bark.
My treehouse.
Branches protecting as I slept in the dark.
Tomorrow after the storm, I will plant another tree and although I will not be here to reap the memories that will be sown, I know that one day, others will.

A JOB is a JOB is a JOB

Gives you spirit, gives you hope, stops you sliding down
endless slope.
Helps you stand on your own.
Forget the look that once was thrown by others with voices full
of scorn.
But as you climb the slippery slope, stretch out your hand,
grasp the chance to escape the spiral of the wicked dance that
tries to tear you every way.
True, it's not the job to hang your wish.
Ten dollars a day, washing dish after dish but.........
A job is a job is a job.

THE VISIT

Just a Chair – leather, old.
Doesn't scare, so why am I frightened to bare my soul?
As private thoughts I'm asked to share to a stranger who listens and tries to heal.
It hurts you know, to show how you feel.
Sadist who enjoys seeing pain, or masochist who'll be back again?
Both of us know I'll be back to sit in the old leather Chair after all it's quite a good fit.
It's where I banish my demons bit by bit.

YOU ARE BETTER THAN THEM

Why is it that you can see further than everyone?
Over the horizon.
Why is it that you can see people for what they are, but others see only when it is too late?
Why is it no one wants to let you remove their blinkers, to expand their world – cure their myopic vision?
Myopia born of timidity and cowardice.
To see, you must first cut free.
From stigma, from the small person with the big job.
The one that blusters and browbeats and cuts you down.
From sycophants who worry for their own thin skins.
Do they not see there is no protection at all, for when the day comes, they'll be the first to fall?
You see further because you are better.
Your course is charted by the needs of others who, like beacons guide you through dangerous currents in an ocean of fear and mediocrity.
Go forward my friend, set your course as others follow.
Stand tall and straight as you go.
You may start alone, but do not waver for in time others will take the path that you show.
The small will always try and pull you down for this is their way.
Ignore them.
They are not destined to be with you as you go forward, straight as an arrow true to your way.

MESS

Grabbing, tugging, clawing, sucking.
So thick I can almost swim.
Impossible to see – plays tricks, light glows pale as senses fail.
All is muffled no sound is clear, but I carry on walking –
swallow my fear.
As I walk through mist, it twists my mind, turns logic blind.
Imagine things – footsteps behind?
Nature's game as I invoke the Holy name.
Then up the hill through evil stew; mans' pollution –
wicked brew.
The sun from high looks on down.
Clears the mist when, with a cry I breathe the air and
mourn the mess.
Why is it we couldn't care less?
I wonder then, if years from now will the mist have gone for
those not yet born?
Will they breathe, or even when they'll ever smile or simply
live and remain forlorn?

VIRUS

Some people – like virus, pernicious, vicious,
their path, their aim, to hurt and maim, and thus destroy so they have a ploy.
You welcome them in – disguised as they are.
Looks just like you when seen from afar and it's OK,
but slowly and surely, they have their own way!
And when it's done and you feel ill, it moves silently on for the next one to kill.
At first, it's all right or that's what it seems.
You play the good host and decide to be nice.
But this thing that's inside won't think twice to take you down as well as your dreams.
But take heart my friend for in the end into hell it will descend, and then to die, like poisonous boil - its plan will foil,
when it bursts and frees you from being sucked dry.
It has a name; you see them at work in all the wrong places
and for some strange reason hold all the aces.
But the day always arrives when people open their eyes and slowly but surely the virus – it dies.

MAN ANT

Ants and man, not hard to compare.
Both scurry about as much as they dare.
Communities all for common good, but at the end of the day it's all about food.
Ants are blind – so what? Have ways to see and get what they got.
Touch and feel, scents mark the track – safely there and quickly back.
It blindly goes on mission bent, almost seems like heaven sent.
Now, look again at him the man – often scurries, no concrete plan.
He too, follows the scent to blindly go where smell of money tells him so.
He watches others, they do the same – all in a race to win the end game.
Looks over his shoulder, checks who's in front, as one by one, all fall prey to the inglorious hunt.
The ant would shudder at this kind of blind, the bile man swallows – his anguished mind, full of stress and endless strife.
The ant has it too so we're really the same because at the end of the day it's a zero-sum game.
We both come and both go but what did we show?

FREEDOM

Whirling, twisting through the air, what a thrill – just watch
for eagle looking to kill.
Riding invisible roads going who knows where, birds soar high
as only they dare.
Masters to go wherever they care.
Past all kinds of magical cumulus clouds, earth covered below
in wisp like shrouds.
Roller coaster, pure joy of it all.
As they look down can they, do they, share the dreams of man
who would sell his soul to whirl and twist, and with the flick of
a wrist do as they can?

NOWHERE TO GO

So early in the day – trapped with nowhere to go.
He took the last seat next to me on the bus.
I see others out of the corners of their eyes.
They seem to be saying 'Tough luck mate.'
Nowhere to go as the warm smell of his breath embraces and hugs like an old friend.
Scent of fermented barley and hops stirs long lost memories.
It's been a long time since I too trapped someone on a bus and took the last seat.
A long time since I too woke up in the gutter and fell onto a bus vowing never again.
It is so easy to stop. I have done it so many times but it's so hard to look at yourself.
Nowhere to go to, trapped till my stop and then break free of the terrible embrace that threatens to ruin and laugh in my face.
Nowhere to go till I welcome my group and tell of the challenge and winning today's race.
Still fighting the years when I too trapped someone on this bus, and he had nowhere to go.

COWBOY STORY

Riding along carrying the load, sure as hell it's a long long road
with dust in my mouth, travelin' south.
Got no money, that's the price to pay for being in the saddle all
of the day.
But I got me my pride and that's a long ride when all I want is
to hit the hay.
Don't mend no fences, ain't no desperado, just ride the trail –
no bravado, just follow the herd till we hit the town.
Then to the saloon, pain to drown with bottle of rye that don't
hide the lie,
no one will care when I lay down and die.
Truth is hard, as hard as my life, never a chance to find me a
wife.
To settle down, to share the day, but who would have me?
It just don't pay.
So, I marry my sorrow and on the morrow with shoulders
heavy, I'll carry the load alone in the saddle, ridin' the road.
More dust in my mouth, keep on south.
Driving cattle – my only friends; hooves poundin' the ground.
One day it'll end, and that's when you'll see a small sad
mound with no one around to read the priests' writing, nice
and neat.
Here lies a man with dirt on his feet.

SNOWFLAKE'S TALE –WWI

Impossible to count.
We shuffle forward row after row ready for glory as heroes all,
we jump spinning and tumbling and slowly fall.
I feel the wind rush as downwards I go, where will I land? – I don't really know.
It's the roll of the dice – Lady Luck's call.
I land, safe and intact – nothing stops me when I start to look back.
I am one of the lucky ones.
Along with the others I land on the hill with hardly a thought for fates terrible kill.
Blown into pools stained a dark dark red, sparkling now with the blood of the dead.
Within minutes we've covered that bloody red hill, its poppies a memory just waiting until....
Pristine and pure, we cover the ground, sheets of white silk snow killing the sound of the scream and the moan.
Cries that will never ever reach home, as quiet and still under our weight, they finally pass, through Heaven's Gate.

SPARE A DIME

Spare a dime?
Hand snakes out – covered in grime.
Skeleton – dressed in skin, every day always the same.
Never looks at your eye.
Better to die?
Sins of man sound in his broken voice.
'I took the wrong road, made the wrong choice.'
Spare a Dime?
The hand, is it real?
Do you feel? Does your heart reach out?
Does it make you ask as you shout?
'How does this happen?'
Once a child carefree and wild, with laughter on lips he played with friends. Didn't see the dark shadow of how it would end.
Spare a Dime?
Does it make you feel good?
Will he just drink it or go get some food?
Will I give him my dime?
The two of us stand there but only one feels the pain, and tomorrow we'll do it all over again.
Different roads, as mine leads home but his trail of grief wears him down to the bone.
Bent almost double under thick matted hair that weighs heavy with shame from his total despair.
So, on you go.
Give him your dime.

BRIGHT LIKE A DIAMOND

Someone's best friend – love story no end.
Hypnotic. Fire. Cold. Hard.
But you don't want to dwell on its story of hell.
It will put you to shame for the story will linger long time after it's left your finger.
Story of blood, of bodies, foul mud.
Just a piece of rock that shines so fine, but don't you know it's got a blood line?
Not of queens or kings but more sinister things.
Of shattered dreams and burning homes hidden now under piles of bones.
Traded and smuggled for the price of a life, this rock of yours that you covet so much.
Look through its facets, see the man on his crutch is it really worth it to have it that much?
So now you know, your diamond so bright, born as it was from the darkness of night.
Wear it with pride for all to see, just don't pretend you didn't know.
Diamond bright, shining so pretty is tainted with blight.
Born as it was in the darkness of night.

RISE UP

You have the power – suppress them all.
They hate you as they cheer you – make them crawl.
Stick in the knife, give it a twist, it's an everyday thing and winning is all.
Mill waiting for grist.
But as night follows day the knife's taken away, and then my friend, that's when you'll pay.
When, where? You'll never know.
As it all spills out – hot lava flow, the hate will engulf you.
There's no stopping the show.
It will soak the parched souls, silence the screams, as freedom blooms from the tears and the dreams.
Finally, you drown and get washed away for the masses have spoken as they have their day.
But now in their joy as they have the hour, it's them just like you that now have the power.
So how will they see things not seen before?
That's what it's like when you walk through the door.
Will the tide now turn as it did for you, will they now see things from a different view?
No thousand-year reign it's never like that.
As the bell chimes the hour they suppress one and all, as the people cheer they all start to crawl.

SNOWFLAKE'S VISIT

I dropped by out of the blue, brought friends as well.
How long would we stay?
A bit hard to tell but come sunrise we melted away.
We left the snowman and took our leave, to dwell on the
laughter we'd brought – on this, winter's eve.

THE SALMON'S TAIL

Sleek and strong.
On a mission.
With silver tail he pushes on.
The path is clear for those that spawn as he returns to where he was born.
Birth and death, it's all the same – nature's game, not for man to ruin for wicked gain.
To dam the lakes and shrink the river – would he ever?
On he goes with no free will, pulled by nature to fulfill his death, as best he can. That's how it is for those who follow nature's plan.
Not by the hand of man.

NOTHING

Moves silent, no sound.
Hears nothing, save flap of wing as it rises heavenwards.
Cat.
Perfect, soars upwards, caresses bird.
Two dancers in a deadly embrace.
The bird, heard nothing.
Scattered wings – old tattered lace.

DON'T JUDGE A BOOK BY ITS COVER

OK. So, I am not who you want me to be.
I am me.
Every atom of my being screams out to the world.
Look but do not stare, do not judge, don't you dare.
I don't judge you – that's not fair.
Accept me as I am and if you can you'll see what's inside,
you'll see a man.
Different from you, that's what I am.
I don't dance to your tune or sing your song.
Anyway, who are you to make the rule of what's accepted,
right or wrong?
All I ask is don't be cruel.
So think for a second perhaps it's you who can't dance or sing
the song.
And me? I've been right all along.

WRITERS BLOCK

Who cares what they write – is it right?
Wield their pen like a sword.
They cut down those not on their side of right.
Who cares what they write?

IF

If only I could fly.
If only I could jump so high.
Walk on water.
If only.......
If only I had the power to heal.
To feel.
Compassion, empathy, to fix a wrong.
If only.......
If only I could square the circle, catch a dream.
Stand at the end of the rainbow.
Relive lost years, abandon fears, banish tears.
If only.......
To free myself from my world of 'IF' to embrace this life, to live it full.
If only.......
To understand *If Only* is inside my head, and it's for me to decide before I'm dead.
If Only.

SAVIOR

Promises to slay your beast, he'll name his price, have his feast.
Banish evil, ease your pain – who's a pawn in a zero-sum game?
Opens you up, lets you breathe, but once inside he'll never leave.
And just like death one thing you'll find, when he comes to call,
cold knock at the door it's all too clear – its payment in kind.
Who is he, who is this man?
For who does he speak – in whose name?
To invoke, and by magic give you a sign.
Is he the devil or one of his slaves?
At the end of the day, it's one and the same.
Sullied with sin and hungry as well, it's you that he wants to hang high on his line.
The power you give him when he offers to save.
But slowly and surely you dig your own grave.
The aura around him – sulphuric and sour, gets stronger and stronger as it reaches the hour.
And when it arrives, and the clock stops its ticking there's a quiet so loud that muffles like shroud.
The smile on his face; full of malice, now you know what you drank was a poisoned chalice.
The water he gave you, the stuff of life, dried you up and shriveled your soul as you slowly got sucked into a bottomless hole.

As he looks down from over his desk, disdain and disgust are what he does best.
He lifts a finger, stretches a hand, vultures start circling as he conducts the band.
Waiting and circling, eager to feed as you just stand in desperate need.
What else could you do with family to feed?
Look into his eye, it's as cold as can be, but you'll see something he'll never see.
Millions of people, ordinary folks, piled high on the alter and feeding the fire that he constantly stokes.
His master, his god, never tires as the cold of his eyes reflect funeral pyres.
Your credit was good but it's debt that he wants as you start to drown in the flood of his taunts
So, who was your savior now turned so sour when the chime of the clock called out the hour?
Just who did you pray to and pin your hope on?
The worst of them all – the god of Mammon?

TIE RACK

Nobody knew, nobody came.
Hadn't had time – didn't unpack, empty tie rack.
And the tie rack waited.
Nobody knew, nobody came.
Why should they?
And the tie rack waited.
'It's for the best.'
'We'll visit often.'
'Make a friend, it's a new beginning, not the end.'
Moved his tired old life onto the bed, what they would say
once he was dead?
Nobody knew, nobody came.
No new friend, not yet.
And the tie rack waited.
And when they came, they closed his eyes, knew not his name,
lonely men all the same.
And the tie rack waited.

MY PERFECT DAY

I feel the gentle breeze as it plays with me.
It flirts with the trees, caressing each leaf this way and that.
I lie on my back and look up.
Sunbeams do their work and gently warm my face, teasing out freckles – summers' calling card.
Light trickles through green gossamer sheen, pinpricks of heaven, host unseen.
More than the stars?
I close my eyes – hypnotized by the music of the bees as they hum.
An orchestra tuning up ever ready for their next concert.
Senses sharpened, I hear petals unfold, their pollen to give, no sacrifice it's give and let live.
Beating wings as maiden sings.
Farmer pours soil through his hand, plays his part in nature's plan.
I imagine a pool, so cool, gently fed from riverbed.
Deep deep hue – azure blue.
I can see through my pool forever.
I have never felt so calm before.
I wish I could stay but I know I cannot, for if I did how would I be able to appreciate this, my perfect day?

HAPPY BIRTHDAY

So bright – I follow.
Promises so much, feels so right, pinprick of light that cuts through the night.
This is it. My journey begins – butterfly from cocoon but like moth to flame; to quickly consume?
It's as bright as the stars as I slowly emerge, pure of sin I have no fears.
So cold I cry when air pricks skin; a thousand needles as they wipe away tears.
Arms embrace and with no time to rest,
I lay my head at my mother's breast.

LOVERS DANCE

Sun hangs low as it bids farewell.
Moon, ever ready starts her ascent.
Earth, as night watch begins, is spun by unseen hand and pays its respects.
Myriad stars, ever watchful are but eyes that do not see.
Triangle of love enshrined as it is for eternity.

SACRIFICE

'Twas the hour of the rising as she gazed upon his face.
Sun, long departed, had laid its darkness all around.
Moon – benevolent, bestowed her presence on all below, as night lay quiet, covered by snow's pristine grace.
Her eyes beseeched unspoken words as the chosen made to touch her face.
A tender kiss on lovers' tears, as he made his peace to take his place.
He ventured forth on path well worn, step by step to meet his fate, strong and true with steady gait.
Gentle sheet of pristine white swallowed footsteps on this night, as on he went.
Ghost consumed in swirling mist waiting for the devil's tryst.
And where he walked rose deadly teeth, granite mountain gleaming white, polished by the moonlit night.
His path, innocent in its request, called out to him on deadly quest.
Predestined route where no man dare, the moonlight cast down a virgin glare.
And as he went from down below, chilling sound on pure pure snow.
The wolf was calling for it could smell – scent of man of noble soul, as howl now summoned from forest deep – partners all, their hour to keep.
And then as one, with mighty howl they put to flight sentient owl.

On he climbed past the line where tree must stop and nothing
grew, save cold and fear – devil's brew.
On he pressed through mountain pass, granite teeth a fearful
mass.
He cried out loud, but none could hear save icy wind on chill
of fear.
'The wolves' they cried, 'That wicked sound. It stops our
blood, fills with dread.
'Twas devil sent so must be fed to let us sleep safe in our bed.'
On he went through granite teeth, iron will through snow and
hail for the pact once made must never fail.
Then through the storm and on the wind, up rose the howl
from far below as now he faced his final hill.
And all around dark mountain rose, its gleaming teeth and
wicked grin, eager to consume the sin, as on he climbed to
sacred place to lay his soul marked with grace.
When night departed with light of dawn, and sun climbed
high to claim its day it looked down upon sightless eyes, vision
of he who claimed the prize.
That fearful night had banished wolf so told the story
throughout the land by child now born who became a man.
It told of lovers on that night and of the savior and the
sacrifice.

THE LAST DREAM

It is no dream to me, my mermaid.
I sink as far as I dare.
Air, silver balloons released from swollen lips.
My lungs convulse, scream for mercy but I cannot.
At least not yet.
Suspended, I float free with hand outstretched, and unseeing
eye to find my dream.
On blue velvet vale I quickly sink, as mocking tail with golden
hue bids me follow on fateful trail.
Alas, it was no dream to me, my mermaid.

YEAR ZERO

It was the year of the Zero, the old way had gone, also the people who sung the last song.
First went the animals as the land disappeared, then went the fish as the prophets had feared.
Victims of poisons floating unseen.
Finally, people of the Anthropocene.
As the heavens looked down on what had been lost, the angels wept tears.
Healing rain.
Year Zero was born out of creation again.
But now it was different, a world swept clean with no one to mourn the Anthropocene.

AWAKENING

And the gods fought.
Incandescent. Shameless. White.
Lightning bolts tear tortured sky on darkened night as angels cry.
Stratus – sisters in spirit. Altocumulus above trembling ground.
Dark and brooding, unleash their wrath.
Apollo – ever watchful, rides high on backs of brothers both,
Nimbus and Cirrus to carve his path.
And as they fought and heaven sighed – innocent of titan's clash.
As earth convulsed, deep in the cave wide eyes witnessed natures lash.
They huddled close two as one 'till dawn encroached with rising sun then left their cave and turned to east, as with homage given slayed the beast.
Golden orb then banished night - gods wrapped in mist then took flight with proud Apollo to accept their rite.
They had granted mercy on the morn, for with beast now slain they had calmed the storm.

WELCOME HOME

Searching for a place.
Not any old place but the right one.
How will I know?
Trust me, when I get there I'll know.
Fit like a glove, just warm enough, steady rhythm of your heart, same as mine.
I am home at last.

PRESSURE

I was strong –could deal with it.
Drop me in, no sin.
Pressure.
Those before me simply trashed.
Weak, at best ersatz.
Couldn't handle it.
Me? I was made for this.
And now, my turn.
Nothing prepared me, my only thought was not to burn.
Pressure.
It shook me to my very core.
My very essence drained out of me.
I tried but was weak, at best ersatz.
It was then I knew there would be no more.
Pressure.
Roaring monster; express train, ripping through me, my very being stripped away.
Nothing left, not even pain.
Body pierced by a thousand arrows.
Catharsis.
Then I heard the truth about myself.
'Hint of chocolate, nutty flavor, has some depth nice to savor, a good cup of coffee when all's said and done.'

BACK AGAIN

Stabbing pain – not again.
All you did was pick up the lid.
Don't move or pretend, don't think to bend.
Just stand still and pray for the end.
Remember the time when with spine supine,
you arched your back, slung the pack?
But then you were young and didn't think twice now you're
flat on your back using a packet of ice.
Everyone thinks you just want a rest, had a fight with the boss
but without you at work it's a terrible loss.
You promise them all it isn't like that, just need to keep the old
back flat.
After a while when the pain's just a twinge, you promise
yourself no lifting binge.
No heavy lids, only big fluffy pillows as with no regrets and a
heartfelt sigh you use the remote, just don't lift it high.
Terrible thing this old back.
It's not that you planned it, to have an attack so just take it
easy as you lie there sublime, a few weeks rest should be
plenty of time.

BORING

Been there, done that.
All so boring.
I want something new not the same old stew.
Give me the lot, your best shot.
Fire up my mind, go on make my day.
Social networks – always online.
Everyone always has something to say.
Fake name and fake face, no guts to be real but you can't be real in a virtual deal.
So much rubbish, so much junk, all so boring – makes you drunk.
Truth to be told I can no longer feel all the facts from the unreal.
So now I've stopped surfing or bother to look.
I think I'll just read a really good book.

THE SILENCE OF THE WITNESS

From my birth – creation, I have been clothed in many layers.
Of war and of triumph. Of angels, soaring high as man proclaimed his new dawn.
Wasted prayer, victim, slayer.
I have seen and been it all.
Through rise and fall I watch; sentient.
Alas, they do not know their time will come to pass.
This is the way of things.
Brought forth from fire as earth heaved in birth, I claimed my place eternal, a beacon of crowning grace.
I watch mans' army – chariots of death on wings of Hades all blindly led, it is devil made.
It never changes – relentless quest.
This is the way of things.
Stories so old born before time, of gods and of heroes in eternal unrest.
Time marches on with every new dawn.
From ancient Sumeria, and those from the east.
Of Vikings and Romans as well as old Greece.
From the Levant to where the sun never set, I witness man's folly – darkness well met.
From over the sea, and Siberian plain, winds blow cold from icy domain.
And so it goes on as earth spins around, blind to the sights and deaf to the sounds.
As they come, they will go, predictably so,
This is the way of things.

END OF NIGHT

I

As the bell tolled the hour at the retreat of the day, all talk
stopped as they turned to pray.
'Twas the hour of the ghoul and everything bad as a cold, cold
mist subdued the land.
Undead arose and started to dance, willing partners in the
devil's band.
Mud oozed from graves row after row as crypt lids rattled with
nary a sound as sinister mist spread over the ground.
Sun, long departed as if swallowed alive made way for the
moon to claim its dark prize.
It shook off its mantle of gossamer mist and laid it down gently
where lovers dared tryst.
Pale yellow light warmed shivering trees long stripped naked
of old autumn leaves.
Old gnarled branches like fingers outstretched seemed to
shake hands as they greet the undead.
Owl cleaves mist on murderous path silently stalking looking
to grasp.
No one saw the unseen, save for the owl who silently preened.

II

They quickly walked over wet cobbled stone leaving the
village and warmth of the home.
No need to speak for they were as one, two lovers, one
heartbeat, never undone. Memories revisited one by one.
Of fire casting shadows as they sat on the ground,
remembering stories long lost but now found.
They recalled the old times of eyes open wide and a tingle of
fright, keeping close to their mothers and trembling inside, as
flickering flames banished the night.
Hushed voices – tales of the undead, caressing like lullaby as
they slept warm in their bed.
They walked through the mist as there followed behind,
footsteps of a different kind.
Deadlier tryst.
One-time lovers just as they were, now unseen and unheard,
'twas the silent footfall of the undead.

III

They carried on walking so sure of the way, on through the darkness as if it were day.
And as they went with her hand in his, undead tuned fiddles with evil hiss.
Now the time with the devil was almost at hand as unseen conductor stalked the land.
Lovers heard nothing; it was not yet the time.
Smell of sulphur, gentle embrace, evil tendrils, the final grace.
When the mist cleared, and the moon gazed down it found them together on cold stone lover's bed – final home of the undead.
And thus it was with terrible chill, the music now started – deadly pill.
It coursed through their bodies, united as one freezing their blood – never undone.
They had chosen to join those not of this world, and leave it unblemished with loved ones to grieve, and to mourn the young lovers who never received their families blessing or their reprieve.

MENU

It's Nature's way.
Day turns to night, heat to cold, some hide as others grow bold.
Snake tastes air as quiet descends – heavy blanket.
Who'll welcome dawn or meet their end?
Who'll taste hunger or have their fill?
Nature's table – a diners delight to savor the kill.
Wildebeest tremble as Buffalo snort, Croc breaks water to cast a cold stare.
Who will it grace with a blink of its eye, who has he chosen – who will die?
Hysterical laughter, mocking sounds, as scavenger barks – licks bloody red lips and leaves its mark.
King now stirs, lord of his pride.
Together they stalk with no need to hide.
Menu?
It's for fate to decide.
Leopard slinks to take by stealth, as with razor fangs finds untold wealth.
In the pale light of moon – animal tracks, slithering trails of armored tails as monsters fight over bloody red snacks.
Meerkat – snug in burrow, but never still for the snake can sense with reptilian skill.
On Elephant feet poison barb makes its mark, but Scorpion looks for easier prey.
Under their weight branches bend as in the dark Vultures dream and patiently wait near freshly killed scene, bloodied red feathers eager to preen.

Garbage collectors one and all, they listen out for Jackal's call.
Raucous sounds fill the air as myriad wings banish night and
take to sky in glorious flight to claim the day.
Predator and prey.
Who had survived and who had not, was ever sparked such a
thought?
Yet come the eve as earth spins free, on the ground or in the
tree, the story starts yet again for those who'll live and those
who'll die.
It's Nature's way.

CROWNING GLORY

Call me what you will.
But to be honest, I do one thing, and that's to kill.
Sorry, but it's what I do.
Not so subtle my cousin the Flu, feel bad after a day or two –
it's not my style.
I'll wait inside you for a while as you walk your lonely mile.
As you hugged, shook unwashed hand, then touched your face
my dream came true.
You delivered to me the ultimate coup.
You can stay inside as much as you want but I'll still be there
ready to taunt.
I'm a virus you know, and can change my style, helps me linger
for quite a while.
Sent by the devil or created by God?
Let the priests interpret what may be said.
But you don't care as you tremble in bed.
You'll mourn your loved ones, those that passed, reflect on
questions they had asked.
The answer is simple – reset the world, don't let it sink,
take time to mourn but also to think.
I'm just a symptom with no quick fix, not cast in stone or
holy ink.
Don't you know? It's natures game – no holy writ that honors
man, graced as he is with the power to think.
Its winner takes all, big or small – man can stumble and head
for a fall.

But I'll be honest, if there's no one left to hear birds sing,
I can easily live in some other thing.
So, drop the arrogance destroyer of all, and me?
Perhaps I am your wake-up call.

PRAYER

Ghostly lamplight.
Softly filtered by nature's shroud, mist caresses – drapes all around.
Embraces with gentle touch.
Like drowning man searching for his final breath, here and there soft light escapes as gossamer tendrils slowly dance.
Unseen, forlorn, lonely moon looks on down as best it can, but street stays silent on the hour with no brave soul to spare a glance.
No welcome light off cobbled stone, families huddle in simple home.
As silence crawls throughout the town, families pray.
It's mankind's way.

ECSTASY

Haven't felt like this in years.
Tingle of anticipation, on edge.
Delicious.
I can't help but look at the vision lying in front of me.
So innocent and pure, I am unsure.
What to do?
How shall I start, to anticipate the end?
It's always the same when pen hits paper.
Shape the page to my will – would I could write on parchment with quill.
For then, once written, never forgot.
The lines that I shape, they are me.
Through the window of the page, I open my soul.
As you read, look through my window.
The view – big or small, lie down or stand tall, walk for a day or all of your life.
My words.
Tread lightly my friend as you welcome each one, for once written it is never undone.

THROUGH MY EYES

Panting, straining, always pulling.
Why can't you let me go?
Trust me – I had some training.
Problem is you don't think like I do.
Hear better, run faster, don't talk about scent – won't embarrass or drool in front of a friend.
Won't jump in the water or shake myself dry, I'll pull if I can – can't blame if I try.
Give me my freedom to run, to bark, get to my tree – make my mark.
There's a world down here in front of my nose; smell of grass, tracks of cat.
Old bone long hidden in time gone by, go on slip the lead, please let me fly.
But it's just a dream, and I know it won't be, my job – to protect for it's me that can see.
And you? You're just human, imperfect at best, can't see what I can or move with my sense.
So how would you manage if I don't guide you around?
I'll see you back home you know that I will.
Take a chance with me now it's the time to be bold.
Slip my lead before I'm too old.

GAME

Snug in hand, unknowing.
Innocent – power ready to unleash.
As day follows night some behold an inglorious sight.
Others lick lips and prepare for the fight.
Never please all as victor looks on – king, lording over vanquished pawn.
A flick of wrist then open fist.
Edge trips on air and spins around, deadly silence 'till gold hits ground.
A thousand heads that pray and sigh had followed the spin as it climbed on high.
Then, with zenith reached and nary a cry it slowly returned – gift of the gods from out of the sky.
They had decreed who would have first kick as many bemoaned their treacherous trick.
Positions taken – guns at dawn.
Now it begins.
Game On.

VINI VIDI VICI

He came to see – conquer it all.
Greeks, Romans, ancient omens.
To touch and relive the glorious past, imagine heroes not destined to last.
Of columns and arches that witnessed great marches.
Of armies and kings, noises of horses and dragons with wings.
As you show him the sites his eyes light up with glee, you unlocked his mind – let it run free.
You've taken him there even more than he wanted as his craving for more leaves you undaunted.
Fulfillment of dream – glorious tours.
You've made his day, and he, yours.

FINISHED SYMPHONY

Bars all around hide the sound.
I must break free – soar.
Free myself.
No Icarus, fly as high as I can.
Alas, locked strong by treble clef, unyielding.
I look through my bars.
Infinite vista rolling unstopped, ending only where thoughts are blocked.
I break the bars to make my mark.
Ever upwards, through the angels as they sigh as clef springs free.
My notes float.
Rejoice the sound now heaven bound.

THE END OF THE RAINBOW

Glorious arc, full of promise for those below.
A time for hunting, peel back layers.
Eternal quest – unanswered prayers.
The Pot of Gold.
From the time of the gods and dreams to behold, relentless search.
The Pot of Gold.
Sky – azure blue after angel's tears that proclaimed the promise – allayed man's fears.
Glorious rainbow for all to behold for those who would dream of,
The Pot of Gold.
Spectrum of light, ready to fight like warriors of old, those who would claim,
The Pot of Gold.
As quest went forth from forest to sea, from all four corners wherever maybe, sentinel guards stood strong in their hold against those who would covet,
The Pot of Gold.
Sisyphean quest as with outstretched hand they roamed the land, armed with stories often told of those who would claim,
The Pot of Gold.
But colors stood strong in the face of the quest, glorious spectrum that never knew rest as they followed the arc just out of reach, they never did learn from those eager to teach.
Repelling those who ventured forth, armed with legends all well told of those who claimed,

The Pot of Gold.
So it was since time gone by – Holy Grail doomed by legend to always fail.
Then came the time – quest fulfilled as he alone finally killed those legends old, and claimed his prize,
The Pot of Gold.
He knew of no color.
No vision of orange, nor yellow or red. No violet or green, embraced with blue on indigo bed.
He saw but grey on sky so cold, as sentinels melted, leaving behind,
The Pot of Gold.

YOUR MEAT, MY POISON

Your prayer, my curse.
My curse, your prayer.
We'll never hear as we both shout, do the math's – they cancel out.
My black, your white.
My white, your black.
Would we could see all mankind – colorblind.
Testaments, Old and New.
Koran or Sanskrit, just who is it that you pray to?
All depends on your point of view.
Old was young.
Young gets old.
Never early, never late to listen to those stories told.
Some shed tears, some have dry eyes.
Some crave the praise – don't criticize.
Short or tall, fat or thin.
Why don't we see who's in the skin?
Some are rich but poor in spirit.
Some are poor but rich in spirit.
Some give hope, a reason to live.
Some hope to get from those that give.
Some always smile – ray of light.
Some never smile –it's always night.
Some breathe pure air, some breathe foul.
Half the world awakes to brave new day.
Half the world closes eyes to welcome night.
Day meets night.

Night meets day.
There's always a time when you can pray.
World.
There's only one so make it last.
By all means, plant your flag upon the ground just make a space for others around.
A done deal or can man change?

OWL

Objective is good.
Intellectual food.
Subjective?
Play detective.
De gustibus non est disputandum.

www.ingramcontent.com/pod-product-compliance
Ingram Content Group UK Ltd.
Pitfield, Milton Keynes, MK11 3LW, UK
UKHW041849190726
13854UKWH00002B/797

9 789655 779028